# A SAILOR'S DICTIONARY

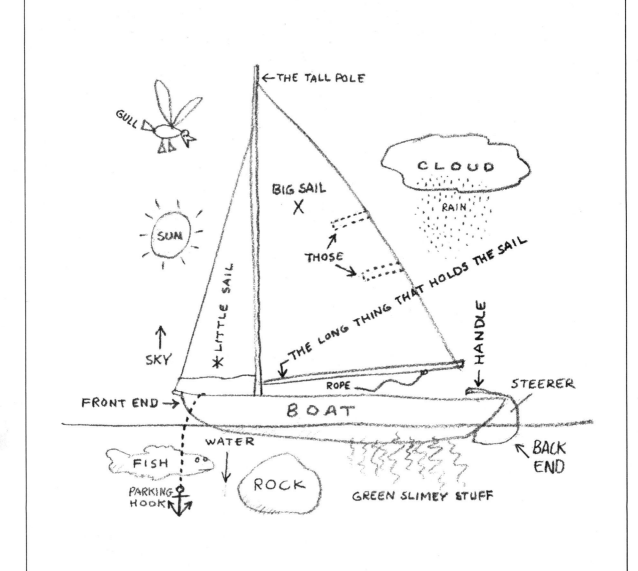

# sailing

## A SAILOR'S DICTIONARY

### BY HENRY BEARD
### & ROY McKIE

WORKMAN PUBLISHING
NEW YORK

Library of Congress Cataloging in Publication Data

Beard, Henry.
    Sailing : (sa ling), n.  1.  the fine art of getting wet and becoming ill while slowly going nowhere at great expense.

        1.  Sailing—Dictionaries—Anecdotes, facetiae, satire, etc.   2.  Yachts and yachting—Dictionaries—Anecdotes, facetiae, satire, etc.   3.  Sailing—Anecdotes, facetiae, satire, etc.   4.  Yachts and yachting—Anecdotes, facetiae, satire, etc.
I.  McKie, Roy.   II.  Title
GV819.B36   1981          797.1′24′03          80-54621
ISBN 0-89480-158-9
ISBN 0-89480-144-9 (pbk.)

Produced by Edward T. Riley.

*Cover and book design:* Paul Hanson

Workman Publishing Company
1 West 39 Street
New York, New York 10018

Manufactured in the United States of America

20   19   18   17   16   15

To all those who have heard the call of the sea.

Aglub:
Condition to be
Avoided (see A-)

# A

| | |
|---|---|
| **A-** | Nautical prefix indicating condition or direction. Thus, a boat that is drifting is *adrift* and something off the side of a boat is *abaft*. Some other common examples of this form: *abash* (toward another boat); *awhiff* (toward an area of low tide); *aglub* (sinking); *aduff* (seated); *adaft* (mentally unbalanced); *asludge* (in an oil slick); *abarf* (under the weather); and *amuck* (caught in mud). |
| **Abandon** | 1. Wild state in which a sailor acquires a boat. 2. Wild state in which a sailor relinquishes a boat. |
| **Achernar** | Navigational star. *See* ZUBENELGENUBI. Did you turn to the back of the book? You did? And the entry under Zubenelgenubi referred you right back here, didn't it? Good. Now, turn back to Zubenelgenubi, then turn back here, then back again to Zubenelgenubi—in fact, go back and forth about a dozen times as quickly as you can, and then read on. Have you done that? Excellent! You've just had a demonstration of the three most vital elements in sailing. First, the rapid flipping of the pages produced a slight movement of the air, and it is just that kind of movement, or "wind," that propels sailboats. Second, since you presumably planned to read through this book in some order—either back to front or front to back—you had to keep going, at least part of the time, in a direction you didn't want to go in. In sailing, this is called "tacking," and going in a direction you don't want to go in a lot of the time is what sailing is all about. Third, in flipping back and forth through the book—it was a little ridiculous, wasn't it?—you were following instructions that you instinctively knew were pointless and silly, given by someone |

Alcohol Stove:
Wintertime Operation

whose judgment you had no reason whatsoever to respect. And blind obedience to absurd requests is absolutely essential in sailing. Welcome aboard, mate! You have the makings of a fine sailor!

| | |
|---|---|
| **Admiralty Law** | Convoluted body of law which regulates behavior at sea. For example, under admiralty law, captains may perform marriages at sea, but not divorces, bar mitzvahs, or most forms of brain surgery; the eating of one individual on a lifeboat to sustain the lives of the others is permissible under some circumstances, but certain recipes, such as casseroles and all but a few cold dishes, are forbidden; and although it is considered improper for a captain to maroon his passengers on some godforsaken island inhabited by unpleasant natives, this stricture does not apply to Ireland or Bermuda. |
| **Alcohol Stove** | Compact stove used in small-boat galleys to bring liquids to body temperature and solid foods to cabin temperature, usually within one hour. Preferred over propane stoves by many boat owners since, in a pinch, its propellant may be served as a cocktail. Alcohol stoves are also used sometimes by boat owners, together with a valid insurance policy, to convert their craft into a liquid asset. |
| *American Practical Navigator* | Ancient nautical treatise, generally thought to deal with navigation, which to the present day has resisted all attempts to decipher it. Often found on board ship as a decorative element or paperweight. |
| **Anchor** | Any of a number of heavy, hook-shaped devices that is dropped over the side of the boat on the end of a length of rope and/or chain, and which is designed to hold a vessel securely in place until (a) the wind exceeds 2 knots, (b) the owner and crew depart, or (c) 3 A.M. |

| | |
|---|---|
| **Anchorage** | 1. Destination at day's end. Always found at the junction of two charts, in the gutter of a chart book, or on a chart not aboard. 2. Any location on the water where at least twenty boats may be accommodated in sufficient proximity to one another so that a sound of 10 decibels (roughly equal to the noise produced by folding a paper towel in half) made by a member of the crew of any one boat may be heard clearly by a person of average hearing on any one of the other boats. |
| **Anchoring** | A process during which the anchor is lowered, and rancor is heightened. |
| **Aneroid Barometer** | Meteorological instrument which sailors often use to confirm the onset of bad weather. Its readings, together with heavy rain, severe rolling, high winds, dark skies, and a deep cloud cover, indicate the presence of a storm. |
| **Approved Abbreviations** | A method of chart-labeling adopted by the U.S. Coast Guard as a means of producing significant cost savings in the printing of charts by eliminating all vowels and every third consonant from descriptive terms. |
| **Auxiliary** | Any object, animate or inanimate, which is in the way when it is not needed and missing or broken when it is. |
| **Aye-Aye** | Somewhat-somewhat redundant-redundant nautical-nautical method-method of-of saying-saying "yes." |

# B

| | |
|---|---|
| **Bar** | Long, low-lying navigational hazard, usually awash, found at river mouths and harbor entrances, where it is com- |

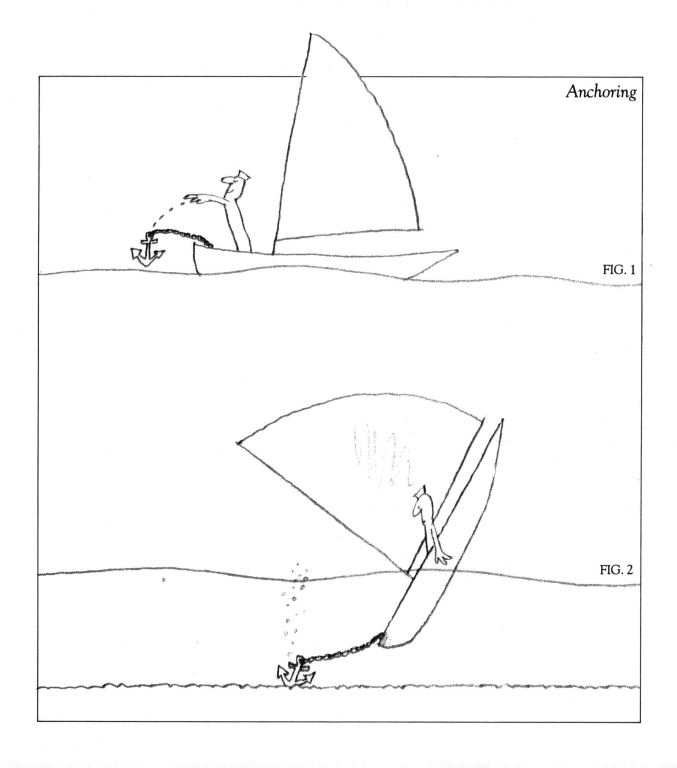

FIG. 1

FIG. 2

Basic Boat Without Options

posed of sand or mud, and ashore, where it is made of mahogany or some other dark wood. Sailors can be found in large numbers around both.

| | |
|---|---|
| **Basic or Stripped Boat** | A term commonly used by boatbuilders and salesmen to describe what is specifically covered in the advertised price of a boat. The basic boat normally consists of several hundred gallons of fiberglass resins and glue, a hundred or so sheets of marine plywood, a ton or more of lead and steel, a sewing kit, and an instruction book. By contrast, the basic boat with options and in "sailaway condition"— a somewhat more expensive proposition—boasts a host of convenient extras, such as a deck, a cabin, an engine, a galley, an anchor, a tiller or wheel, a rudder, and a cockpit; and sails, spars, rigging, fittings, and portholes. |
| **Battery** | Electrochemical storage device capable of lighting an incandescent lamp of a wattage about equal to that of a refrigerator bulb for a period of 15 minutes after having been charged for 2 hours. |
| **Beam Sea** | A situation in which waves strike a boat from the side, causing it to roll unpleasantly. This is one of the four directions from which wave action tends to produce extreme physical discomfort. The other three are *bow sea* (waves striking from in front), *following sea* (waves striking from the rear), and *quarter sea* (waves striking from any other direction). |
| **Berth** | Any horizontal surface whose total area does not exceed one half of the surface area of an average man at rest, onto which at least one liter of some liquid seeps during any 12-hour period and above which there are not less than 10 kilograms of improperly secured objects. |

*Boarding*

WRONG METHOD OF BOARDING #1.

WRONG METHOD OF BOARDING #2.

WRONG METHOD OF BOARDING #3.

| | |
|---|---|
| **Bilge** | Strictly speaking, the lowest spaces inside the hull where poorly understood chemical reactions among the liquids which collect there create a slow-moving, viscous substance which some scientists believe is a primitive form of life; but now, more commonly, the substance itself. |
| **Binoculars** | Entertaining shipboard kaleidoscope which when held up to the light reveals interesting patterns and designs caused by salt spray, thumbprints, and scratches. Uncapped, its lenses may also be employed to collect small amounts of salt from seawater through evaporation. |
| **Bitter End** | One of only eight names authorized by the Coast Guard for establishments serving alcoholic beverages in harbor areas. The other are: The Outrigger, The Beachcomber, The Hatch, The Rusty Rudder, The Crow's Nest, The Jolly Roger, and Barnacle Bill's. |
| **Boarding** | The knowledgeable sailor does not "get on" a boat or "climb in" a boat—he *boards* a boat. And the prudent individual does not "stay behind," "keep off," or "say the hell with it"—he *remains ashore*. |
| **Boat Haul-out** | An annual procedure during which a boat owner's collection of marine specimens is removed from his hull, usually by convicts in work-release programs. Electronic gadgets, binoculars, radios, and other costly bric-a-brac which have gradually encrusted cabin spaces over the year are removed as well, and at most boatyards, as part of the operation, the boat owner is also thoroughly cleaned out by professionals. |
| **Bobstay** | Tiny seabird with an annoying warble disturbingly similar to the whining sound made by a metal cable parting: *SNIK weeeeeeeeeee bee-WINGGG!* |

**Boom**
1. Laterally mounted pole to which a sail is fastened. Often used during jibing to shift crew members to a fixed, horizontal position. 2. The sound produced when an alcohol stove is used to convert a boat into a liquid asset.

**Boomkin**
The sound that accompanies the conversion of a small boat, such as a dinghy, into a liquid asset.

**Bosun's Chair**
Nineteenth-century nautical execution device consisting of an iron chair to which a lightning rod was attached. The condemned sailor was strapped into the bosun's chair where he remained until a fortuitous bolt of lightning or a lethal dose of St. Elmo's fire resulted in his execution.

**Bottom**
The land under the water. Its characteristics are indicated on nautical charts to assist sailors in anchoring. Some common types of bottom which boatmen are likely to encounter are: ick, ycch, ugh, crddy, crppy, ftd, rttn, nsty, awfl, hrrbl, dsgstng, and unblvbl.

**Brightwork**
Mental effort through which the more intelligent individuals on board ship evade their share of boring and unpleasant tasks, such as polishing brass hardware.

**Bulkhead**
Discomfort suffered by sailors who drink too much.

**Bunk**
Nautical lore.

**Buoy**
Navigational aid. There are several types and colors of buoys of which the most numerous are: the black can (seen as a fuzzy black spot on the horizon); the red nun (seen as a fuzzy black spot on the horizon); the red or green day beacon (seen as a fuzzy black spot on the horizon); and the vertically striped black-and-white channel marker (seen as a fuzzy black spot on the horizon).

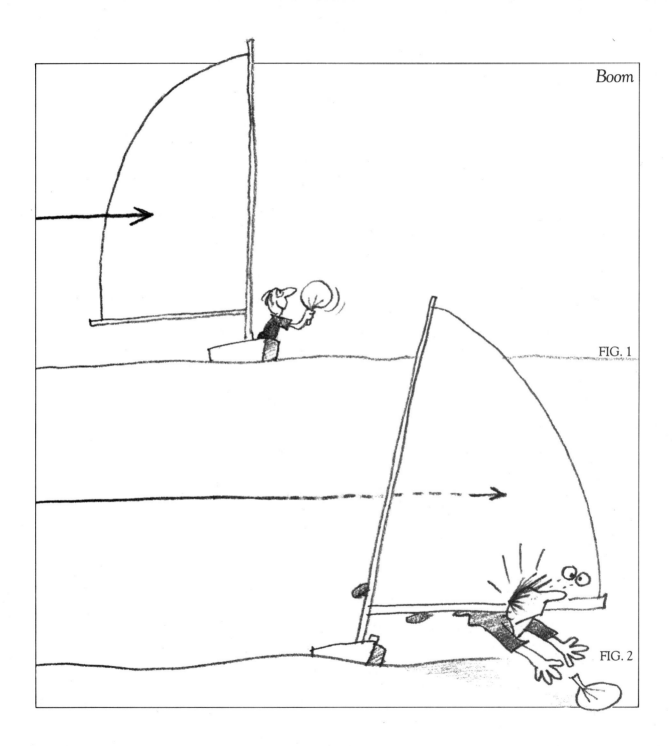

*Boom*

FIG. 1

FIG. 2

| **Burdened Vessel** | The boat which, in a collision situation, did not have the right-of-way. *See* PRIVILEGED VESSEL. |

# C

| **Cabin** | A cramped, closetlike compartment below deck where crew members may be stored—on their sides if large or on end if small—until needed. |
| **Calm** | Sea condition characterized by the simultaneous disappearance of the wind and the last cold beverage. |
| **Canvas** | An abrasive sailcloth used to remove excess skin from knuckles. |
| **Capsize** | The interior diameter of any piece of headgear, usually expressed in inches. |
| **Captain** | *See* FIGUREHEAD. |
| **Catalog** | A list provided by manufacturers of items that are currently unavailable, or that have been dropped from production entirely. |
| **Catamaran** | A boat design involving the use of two joined hulls. Its chief features are that it is twice as likely to hit something or develop a hole or leak, but will generally take double the amount of time to sink after having done so. |
| **Caulk** | Any one of a number of substances introduced into the spaces between planks in the hull and decking of a boat that give a smooth, finished appearance while still permitting the passage of a significant amount of seawater. |
| **Centerboard** | Permanently jammed movable keel. |

*Burdened Vessel*
*Failing to Give Way*

Charterer with Chart

| | |
|---|---|
| **Chantey** | Traditional sea song, like "Skeg o' My Heart," "My Darling Brigantine," "Try to Remember the Kind of Sub Tender," and "Catch a Falling Spar." |
| **Chart** | 1. A large piece of paper that is useful in protecting cabin and cockpit surfaces from food and beverage stains. 2. A common decorative motif on place mats. 3. A nautical map that assists the boatman in determining whether he is on the water (blue on charts) or on land (yellow). |
| **Chart Compasses** | An instrument consisting of two hinged legs, one holding a pencil, the other terminating in a sharp point, that is used to describe on charts the circles sailboats customarily travel in. |
| **Charter** | Chartering agencies operate quite openly in the "red-buoy" districts of most harbors. They offer "bare-boats," "cat-boats," "jolly-boats," and other "aweigh-for-pay" craft, and if you have the "jack"—$100 per day and up—it's "Hello, sailor!" |
| **Chip Log** | Following a rash of extremely unpleasant incidents in the 1960's, the Coast Guard has required boat owners to maintain a daily record of snack consumption to insure an equitable division among guests and crew of a large category of "munchable provender" whose presence on board ship has been deemed to be a potential source of disputes likely to result in the commission of a felony. |
| **Chock** | Sudden and usually unpleasant surprise suffered by Spanish seaman. |
| **Chronometer** | Precision instrument which registers sharp impacts by displaying a telltale spiderweb pattern on its glass face, by the absence of a normal ticking sound when held to the |

Clothing: Types of Foul Weather Gear

SOU-WESTER                    NOR-EASTER

ear, or by the presence of small, loose pieces moving around within its case when shaken. It also indicates excess humidity by forming tiny droplets on the inside of its face, and when stopped, it displays the correct time twice each day.

| | |
|---|---|
| **Circuit Breaker** | An electromechanical switching unit intended to prevent the flow of electricity under normal operating conditions and, in the case of a short circuit, to permit the electrification of all conductive metal fittings throughout the boat. Available at most novelty shops. |
| **Citizen's Band/ Marine Radio** | Part of a government study of terrestrial radio emissions to determine if intelligent life exists on earth. None has so far been detected. |
| **Clew** | Evidence leading to recovery of a missing sail. |
| **Clothing/Foul Weather Gear** | Type of weatherproof clothing usually needed only in the fall, spring, winter, and summer months. |
| **Clouds** | Concentrations of water vapor at various levels of the atmosphere, the shapes and sizes of which are often used in predicting weather changes. Thus, a cloud shaped like an umbrella indicates rain, while one shaped like a beach chair indicates sunny weather. |
| **Clove Hitch** | Any of a number of difficulties encountered in the use of this popular spice. |
| **Club, Yacht Club, Racing Association** | Troublesome seasonal accumulation in coastal areas of unpleasant marine organisms with stiff necks and clammy extremities. Often present in large numbers during summer months when they clog inlets, bays, and coves, making navigation almost impossible. Among their |

unpleasant characteristics are an unmistakable loud, braying cry and a vicious competitiveness which is at its peak among their young. The infestations are most serious along the coasts of Connecticut, Massachusetts, and Maine. They can be effectively dislodged with dynamite, but, alas, archaic federal laws rule out this option.

| | |
|---|---|
| **Cockpit** | Open area in the stern from which a sailboat is steered toward the desired destination. |
| **Cocktails** | The desired destination. |
| **Code** | 1. Regular form of static heard on marine radios, often referred to as "Morse." 2. Relatively mild upper respiratory ailment commonly contracted at sea. |
| **Codfish** | Popular dish on seafood restaurant menus where it appears under a variety of names, including haddock, scallops, bluefish, swordfish, and lobster Newburg. |
| **Coiled** | 1. Arranged in a neat circular pattern. 2. Relatively mild upper respiratory ailment commonly contracted at sea by sailors from Brooklyn. |
| **Collision** | Unexpected contact between one boat and another. As a rule, collisions that result in the creation of two smaller and less seaworthy vessels from the hull of one are thought to be the most serious. |
| **Colorful Nautical Tidbits/the Half-model** | A traditional time-saving design tool of naval architecture, consisting of the lengthwise half of a hull-form which incorporates the basic shape and lines of a vessel. Historically, its employment by boatbuilders unfamiliar with the basic concept led to considerable delay in its wider acceptance since the first half-ships constructed from half-models sank immediately after launching. |

*Cocktails: Resupply*

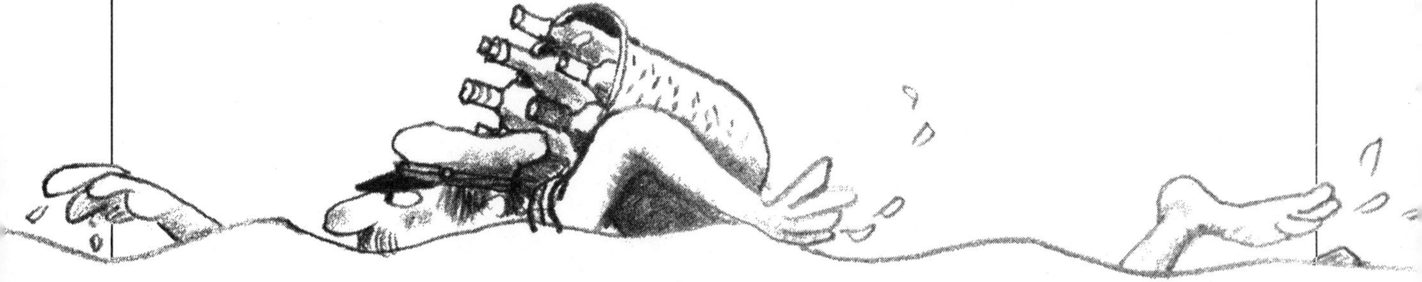

| | |
|---|---|
| **Compass** | Navigational instrument that records a variety of directional errors and indicates the presence of machinery and magnets on board ship by spinning wildly. |
| **Compass Points (Boxing the Compass)** | Many boat owners have learned to vent their frustrations on their compasses and get some exercise at the same time by taking up compass boxing. Heavily padded gloves reduce the risk of damage to the instrument or injury to the sailor. Points are scored whenever the compass needle makes a full 360-degree spin. Professional compass boxing was once popular in maritime areas, and in its heyday, compass "cards" featured such greats as Kid Azimuth and "Gentleman Gimbal" Morrison, but after several well-publicized "compass fixes" in which fighters concealed magnets in their gloves and compasses were set to "take a spin," the sport went into a long decline. |
| **Compass Rose** | Sobriquet given to Rosemary Alcott (1871–1922), an Englishwoman who somehow became naturally magnetized. She earned a living for a while as a circus and music-hall performer, but after a matinee in Brighton that led to five ships striking rocks off shore and foundering, she was banned—by a special act of Parliament—from all ports and coasts in Britain and the Empire. A sympathetic public took up a subscription to establish her as a seamstress in a village in the geographic center of Kent. After a quiet life, she made the headlines again in March, 1919, when the king decorated her for heroism. It was revealed at that time that for nearly two years she had been working as a British agent in a tailor's shop in Hamburg where she was credited with helping to keep the German fleet at anchor. At her death, every compass in the British Empire was hooded for one hour in her honor. |

*Compass: Emergency Procedure*

Cruising: Arrival

| | |
|---|---|
| **Corps of Engineers** | The promulgation by President Truman in 1949 of the then-secret Executive Order 2395—the Defense Inappropriateness Measures—assigned responsibility for constructing and maintaining canals, channels, and ports to the Army; highway construction to the Navy; railroad operation to the Air Force; and implementation of a national mobile library program to the Marines. The measures were born in a period of anti-Soviet hysteria and were designed to confuse the enemy about the missions and deployments of the various American military forces in time of war. Following the tragic loss of the *Margaret Fuller*, the first and last of a projected class of LSB's (Landing Ship, Books) to be operated by the Marines, calmer heads prevailed, and the order was drastically modified. Today, only the Army, through its Corps of Engineers, retains its incongruous mission. |
| **Course** | The direction in which a skipper wishes to steer his boat and from which the wind is blowing. |
| **Crew** | Heavy, stationary objects used on shipboard to hold down corners of charts, anchor cushions in place, and dampen sudden movements of the boom. |
| **Cross Bearings** | Unusually difficult or trying conditions at sea. |
| **Cruising** | Waterborne pleasure journey embarked on by one or more people. A cruise may be considered successful if the same number of individuals who set out on it arrive, in roughly the same condition they set out in, at some piece of habitable dry land, with or without the boat. |
| **Current** | Tidal flow that carries a boat away from its desired destination, or toward a hazard. |

**Cyclone**

Technical name for storms. Mariners use a universal measure of the severity of storms, called the Beaufort scale, which classifies sea conditions for sailors. The categories—or "forces"—are: 1. No wind at all; 2. Too little wind; 3. Too much wind; 4. Much too much wind; 5. Wind, wind, wind—whoooeee, will it ever stop blowing?; and 6. Blammo!

# D

**Dead Reckoning**

Traditional form of rough-estimate navigation used for hundreds of years by sailors, almost all of whom are dead. As it is practiced today, the technique involves the use of three special "chart darts" which are "entered" in the appropriate region of a nautical chart from 8 feet away. The resulting holes are joined by pencil lines to form a triangle whose central point is taken as the boat's position.

**Deck Lines**

There are a large number of these. Among the most common are: "Do you sail often?"; "How did you happen to get interested in sailing?"; "Here, let me help you with that"; "Would you like a cushion/cocktail?"; and "Want to take the wheel/tiller?"

**Deck Shoe**

A canvas shoe with a rubber sole having a specially designed tread that provides for secure footing on deck unless the deck is wet, the shoe is somewhat worn, the deck is worn, or the shoe is wet.

**Derelict**

In spite of the selfless work of the Salvation Navy, many harbors are still filled with "bum-boats" and "drifters" who "kedge" handouts, usually with some plaintive cry like, "Can you spare ten dollars for a pint of bottom

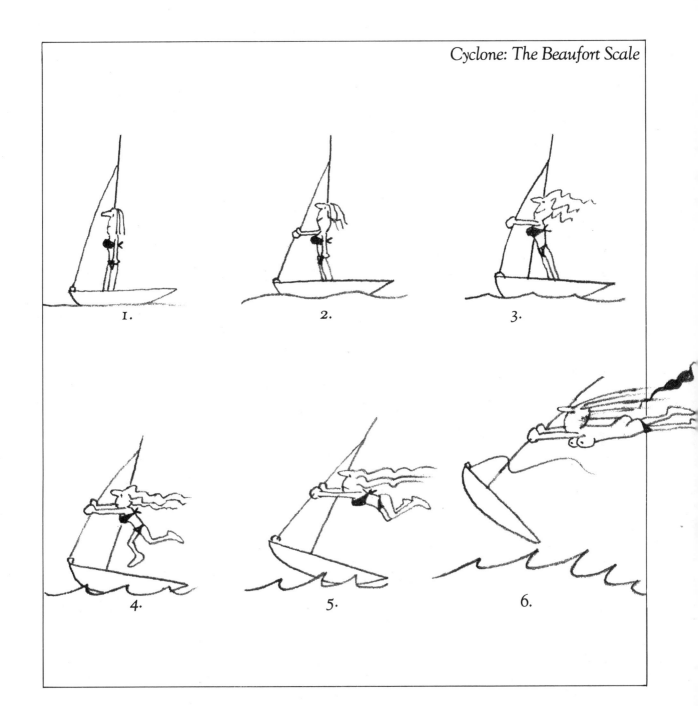

1.

2.

3.

4.

5.

6.

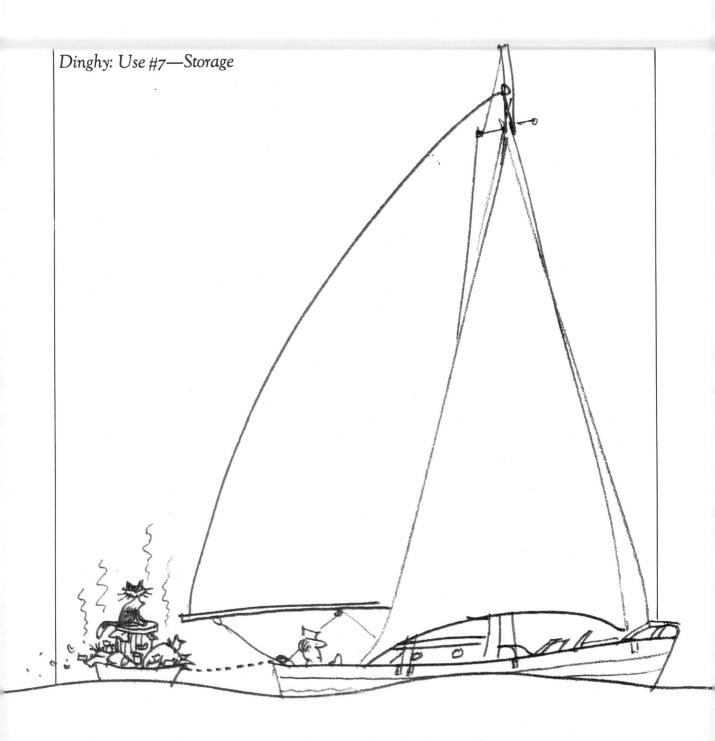

Dinghy: Use #7—Storage

paint?" There is no sadder sight than a yachtsman who has touched bottom, but sometimes a few hearty words of encouragement are enough to put him back on his sea legs, ready to set a course for self-respect. "Listen, kelp-face," you might cry good-naturedly the next time you are accosted by one of these individuals, "why don't you get a job as a piling? There's no charge for the creosote, and if you don't mind sea gulls doing *numero duo* on your noggin, you're home free!" Remember, the sailing fraternity looks after its own.

| | |
|---|---|
| **Deviation** | Unnatural love of the sea. |
| **Dinghy** | Small craft customarily towed from the stern of boats, stowed on deck on larger boats, or stolen from moorings when boats are away. It serves the purpose of lifeboat, shore shuttle, and wastebasket, and by filling up with water and sinking, it provides a crude measurement of recent rainfall. Ideally, it should have sufficient stability to carry the entire crew at least 50 boat-lengths away from their vessel before foundering. For reasons lost in maritime tradition, dinghies—or "dinks" as they are often referred to—are by custom equipped with two oars, but only one functioning oarlock. |
| **Distress Signals** | International signals which indicate that a boat is in danger. For example, in Italian waters: moaning, weeping, and wild gesticulations; in French waters: fistfights, horn-blowing, and screamed accusations; in Spanish waters: boasts, taunts, and random gunfire; in Irish waters: rhythmic grunting, the sound of broken glass, and the detonation of small explosive devices; in Japanese waters: shouted apologies, the exchange of calling cards, and minor self-inflicted wounds; and in English waters: doffed hats, the burning of toast, and the spilling of tea. |

| | |
|---|---|
| **Dock** | Harbor landing-place which goes *squeak* or *thud* when hit. *See* PIER. |

| | |
|---|---|
| **Dolphin** | Marine mammal of legendary intelligence often credited with saving drowning sailors by supporting them and nudging them to shore. Unfortunately, due to the expense of feeding these likable creatures, it has not proved practical to equip boats with life-dolphins. An early attempt to exploit their remarkable qualities ended in tragedy when the S.S. *City of Cadiz*—equipped with twenty-three of the animals—went down off Tenerife in 1923 with all hands, and all fins. A reconstruction of the catastrophe from somewhat hysterical wireless broadcasts sent by the radio operator of the *Cadiz* as it foundered puts the blame for the mishap on the ship's Portuguese chef, who in an ill-advised burst of culinary enthusiasm removed two of the dolphins from their wooden holding tank on the deck of the tiny tramp steamer and featured them in a Seafood Zarzuela. The remaining fish, apparently maddened by the conversion of their companions into a midday meal, became increasingly unruly and ultimately butted the flimsy tank to bits. Its contents flooded the overloaded vessel, which quickly sank. Her owner, one M. Lucien Fichou of Marseilles, had neglected to provide lifeboats for the vessel, reasoning, as he testified to a court of inquiry, that the presence of alternate means of escape would have "shed doubts on the moral fiber and inherent capacities of the dolphins, thus perhaps removing their élan for their appointed task and plunging them into a poisonous gloom in the grasp of which they would have been incapable of performing their duties." Fichou was sentenced to twenty years in the notorious prison on Devil's Island, where, in one of those |

charming oddities that make the study of nautical history so rewarding, he spent much of his time developing an ingenious pressurized bottle designed to permit deep-sea divers to have an aperitif while submerged.

**Double-ender**     Sailboat design in which the shape of the stern closely resembles that of the bow. This design is an advantage when waves are striking the boat from behind, since the sharply pointed stern breaks them smoothly, but in calm waters it is often a source of some confusion for inexperienced boatmen. Painting *front* and *back* in large letters in the appropriate places on a double-ender may be a source of some embarrassment to the novice sailor, but it does eliminate a potential source of piloting error.

**Dry Rot**     Degenerative condition of wood that transforms ship timbers into a substance that has compressive and tensile strengths about equal to those found in coleslaw. Since salt water is the most common cause of dry rot, the best preventive measure is to keep vessels with predominantly wooden construction in a cool, dry place—such as a garage or warehouse—on a permanent basis.

# E

**Emergency**     At sea, an emergency situation is presumed to exist whenever one or more persons find themselves on any floating craft in waters whose depth makes it impossible for the shortest one of them to stand on the bottom and still have his head completely above water.

| | |
|---|---|
| **Engine** | Sailboats are equipped with a variety of engines, but all of them work on the internal destruction principle, in which highly machined parts are rapidly converted into low-grade scrap, producing in the process energy in the form of heat, which is used to boil bilge water; vibration, which improves the muscle tone of the crew; and a small amount of rotational force, which drives the average size sailboat at speeds approaching a furlong per fortnight. |
| **Equator** | A line circling the earth at a point equidistant from both poles which separates the oceans into the North Danger Zone and the South Danger Zone. |
| **Error** | Navigational inaccuracy. "Compass error," a catchall term covering the more or less permanent directional distortions which that instrument is subject to, is the most notable. Attempts are generally made to reduce or eliminate this problem by placing in the vicinity of the compass various devices with corrective properties, such as rabbits' feet, four-leaf clovers, and religious statuettes. |
| **Etiquette** | Marine custom establishes a code of social behavior and nautical courtesy for every conceivable occasion. Thus, for example, a boat belonging to another boatman is always referred to as a "scow," a "tub," or a "pig-boat." When one skipper goes aboard another's boat, he does not hesitate to tell him frankly about any drawbacks or disadvantages he finds in comparison to his own craft. Sailors welcome every opportunity to improve their vessels, and so he knows that his remarks will be greatly appreciated. When one sailboat passes another, it is customary for the captain of the passing boat to make a bladderlike sound with his lips and tongue, and for the captain of the passed boat to return the courtesy by |

*Etiquette:*
*Exchange of Courtesies I*
*(Captain's Compliments)*

Etiquette:
Exchange of Courtesies II
(First Serve)

offering a smart salute consisting of a quick upward movement of the right hand with the second digit extended. There is a time-honored exchange of courtesies involved in boarding ship which sailors who respect nautical conventions always use. Having the proper questions and responses down pat lets others know that you are a full-fledged member of the seagoing fraternity. The person who wishes to board a ship says, "Hey there, on deck, can I come aboard?" to which the skipper—or in his absence, the senior member of the crew—replies, "My compliments [or, the captain's compliments] sir, but hay, as you may not be aware, is for horses." The correct rejoinder to this is, "Oh, come on." Whoever is on board will then insist that the person wishing to enter the ship "preface your remarks, if you would be so good, with the magic word." At this point, the person wishing to board replies, "*Please,* can I come aboard?" and he is then granted permission with the phrase, "With all due respect [or, the captain's respects] sir, I do not know if you *can* or not, but you *may*." There are literally hundreds of different forms of nautical usage, and there is only room here to give a little flavor of the rich traditions of the sea.

# F

| | |
|---|---|
| **Fast** | Firmly attached, as for example, a rope made fast to a piling. Also used to describe a boat that has run aground. Thus, a boat that appears to be unusually slow, may in fact be "fast." Nautical terminology is full of these amusing paradoxes! |
| **Figurehead** | Decorative dummy found on sailboats. |

| | |
|---|---|
| **Fish** | Any living creature that does not call the Coast Guard when faced with the prospect of being submerged for more than one minute. |
| **Fitting Out** | Series of maintenance tasks performed on boats ashore during good-weather weekends in spring and summer months to make them ready for winter storage. |
| **Fix** | 1. The estimated position of a boat. 2. The true position a boat and its crew are in most of the time. |
| **Flag** | Any of a number of signaling pennants or ensigns, designed to be flown upside down, in the wrong place, in the wrong order, or at an inappropriate time. |
| **Flag (Liberian)** | Flag of convenience flown by many merchant ships. It has the advantage that Liberian laws are very loose, and hence the cost of operating a ship under Liberian registry is low, but suffers from the disadvantage that, generally speaking, the Liberian flag is accorded the respect and courtesy one would expect upon displaying a bedspread or pot holder. |
| **Flashlight** | Tubular metal container used on shipboard for storing dead batteries prior to their disposal. |
| **Flipper** | Rubber swimming aid worn on the feet. Usually available in only two sizes, 3 and 17. |
| **Flood** | Sudden rising of water on shore during which "landlubbers" are introduced to the pleasures of boating. |
| **Flotsam** | Anything floating in the water from which there is no response when an offer of a cocktail is made. |
| **Fluke** | The portion of an anchor that digs securely into the bottom, holding a boat in place; also, any occasion when this occurs on the first try. |

| | |
|---|---|
| **Fo'c's'l** | Th' c'b'n f'r'th'st f'r'd. |
| **Fog** | "Oh fatal vapor, thrice accursed brew<br>Thou gloom of doom, thou deadly devil's stew!"<br>— Shakespeare *All Ashore That's Going Ashore, Act III, Scene 1.* |
| **Fuel** | Sailboats without auxiliary engines do not require fuel as such, but an adequate supply of a pale yellow carbonated beverage with a 10 percent to 12 percent alcohol content is essential to the operation of all recreational craft. |

# G

| | |
|---|---|
| **Galley** | 1. *Ancient:* Aspect of seafaring associated with slavery.<br>2. *Modern:* Aspect of seafaring associated with slavery. |
| **Gangway** | On boarding ship, the point of no return. |
| **Gender** | As a rule, boats are customarily referred to as "she," and parts of boats are preceded by "her," but there are a few ports, such as Key West, Fla., and Provincetown, Mass. where "he" and "his" are becoming common. |
| **Gimbals** | Movable mountings often found on shipboard lamps, compasses, etc., which provide dieting passengers an opportunity to observe the true motions of the ship in relation to them, and thus prevent any recently ingested food from remaining in their digestive systems long enough to be converted into unwanted calories. |
| **Gong Buoy** | One of a class of sound-emitting buoys with movable hammers that hit bells or gongs when waves rock them. Buoys not equipped with active means of sound generation also send out characteristic sounds when struck, which help the sailor identify them. The nun and the can |

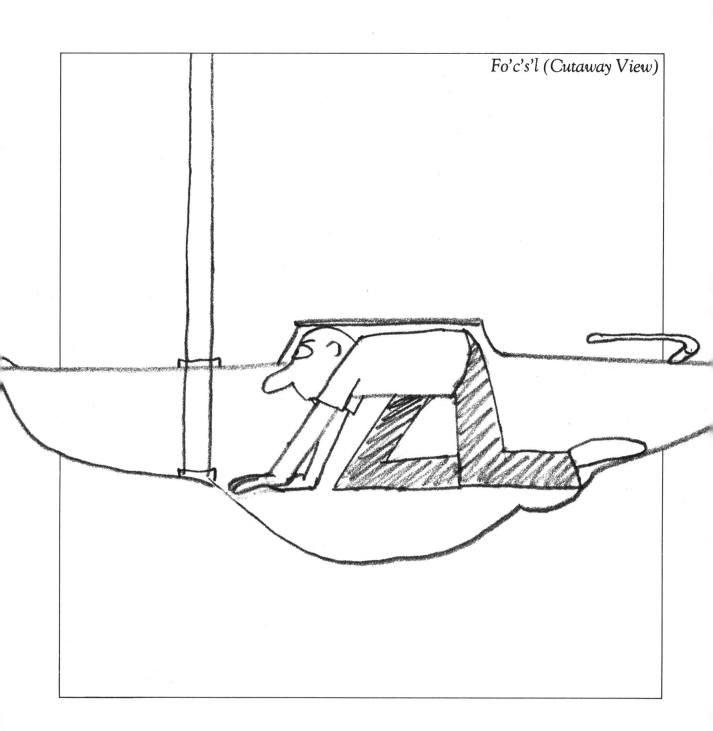

Fo'c's'l (Cutaway View)

emit a sharp *clunk* or *clank*; the day beacon on pilings yields a deep thudding sound with some splintering noises; fixed channel markers surrounded by rip-rap (circles of stones) give off a grating, cracking, or crunching sound; channel-marking stakes produce a light *snap*; and moorings usually make a series of faint tapping noises as they pass along the hull.

| | |
|---|---|
| **Greenwich Time** | The incorrect time in London. |
| **Gunwale** | Upper edge of the side of a boat, pronounced "gunnel," "gunn'l," "gnl," or "gn." By the way, many people have difficulty mastering nautical pronunciation, and this seems as good a place as any to address this problem. The effect to aim for is a cross beween train announcements and the sounds that come from patients in dentists' chairs. Probably the best way to develop a "sea mouth" is to practice speaking with an unopened chowder clam held in your mouth. Work on this sentence: "Gaff that grommet gasket to the garboard gudgeon gunter." It should come out something like: "Gfthtgrmgsktthgbdgdgngnr." Remember, properly delivered nautical commands must be incomprehensible to the person toward whom they are directed even when accompanied by clear hand signals or pantomime indicating the desired action. The U.S. Navy has a handy memory aid for the seven basic rules of the nautical command—it's a good one to memorize:<br>C onfuse<br>O bscure<br>M umble<br>M ispronounce<br>A bbreviate<br>N asalize<br>D rool |

Gunwale (Encumbered)

Hazard (Man-made)

# H

**Hazard**

1. Any boat over 2 feet in length. 2. The skipper of any such craft. 3. Any body of water. 4. Any body of land within 100 yards of any body of water.

**Head**

Technically, the toilet on a boat, although heads are in fact stucturally much closer to the radioactive waste disposal systems which they resemble. A head's operation is rather complicated, but once mastered, it should present no particular difficulty to the boat owner or visitor. Approved methods of working the marine head are contained in the excellent, though somewhat superficial, seven-volume work, *Principles and Operation of the Marine Head*, published by the Department of Defense in cooperation with the Department of Justice and the surgeon general. Also, most manufacturers of shipboard sanitary units provide extensive audiovisual materials on a loan basis to purchasers of their products, and many educational institutions in areas with large boating populations offer a basic 80-hour "hands-on" course in Sanitary Navigation (previous credits in Fluid Dynamics and the Fundamentals of Crowd Control may be a prerequisite). Proper operation of the head is essential. Simply put, the head macerates and chlorinates a certain very restricted class of waste materials prior to discharge, transforming them into a chemical compound that annoys, but does not kill, marine life. *Foreign matter must not be introduced into the head under any circumstances.* Although it operates on the principle of the chain saw—as the noise which accompanies its use suggests—it is highly susceptible to clogging. Heads that become clogged can result not just in considerable inconvenience, but in great

*Heeling: Stage #3*

expense as well, requiring the intervention of trained personnel with decontamination gear and remote-handling equipment, and in extreme—but by no means uncommon—cases, may lead to the abandoning of the boat. (Incidentally, in that regard, most insurance policies specifically exclude clogged heads in their coverage of the boat, or have a high deductible—typically $50,000—for that category of risk.) The key to the operation of the head is the addition at the appropriate moment of a special tablet, a macaroon-sized cake composed of a blend of potassium cyanide, phosgene, lye, prussic acid, formaldehyde, diatomaceous earth, ground glass, metal filings, and high explosive. Though not specifically prohibited by the Geneva convention, these tablets are regulated to some degree by the United Nations; in international waters, it is advisable to consult the various protocols that govern their transport and use.

| | |
|---|---|
| **Heeling** | A basic process affecting all sailboats, which begins with the boat leaning over as the wind presses on one side of its sails, and ends as the sailboat finally exhibits its natural tendency to come to a state of rest on the sea bottom. |
| **Houseboat** | In recent years, there have been a spate of complaints about unscrupulous developers, chiefly in California and Florida, selling "sea-site" vacation homes on "prime ocean-view wet-land water-front-and-back" parcels in developments with names like Wave Crest, Sea Gardens, and Rancho Aguamucho. Caveat emptor! If the fine print in your purchase contract requires you as a homeowner to carry collision insurance and have YMCA swimming certification, you're headed for a tidal rip-off! |

**Hydrophobia**  Fear of the water. Accepted by many states as a basic test of fundamental sanity.

# I

**Iceboat**  A sailboat having such characteristics that it is statistically more likely to crash than to sink; that it can become a total loss without sinking; and that in the event of a mishap, its crew will be able to walk to shore.

**Ice Chest**  Insulated compartment in the galley that holds a block or two of ice to keep food and beverages cool. No one knows why—it could have something to do with sudden temperature changes, continuous sea motion, and pressure—but fresh produce placed inside undergoes a transformation into a dense, peatlike substance surprisingly similar to soft coal; frozen meat corrodes; and containers of beer are somehow transmuted into cans of diet Fanta.

**Inland Waters**  As defined by the Coast Guard, areas of U.S. territorial waters abutting or passing through heavily populated regions, where a man who falls overboard will dissolve before he drowns.

**International Rules**  Set of worldwide maritime agreements that: outlaw excessive noise—such as the slamming of hatches, sounding of loud horns or whistles—in narrow straits, like those of Gibraltar, Molucca, and Hormuz; require ships to have a clean flag and a note signed by the king, president, prime minister, or chairman before leaving port; decree that anything left floating around in the ocean will be thrown out or given away; and, in the Panama and Suez canals, prohibit ships from "racing" up and down the locks.

*Ice Chest: Routine Maintenance*

# J

**Jetsam**

Too often shipboard refuse is unceremoniously dumped over the side with no attention whatsoever to the nautical niceties. That pile of untidy refuse in the bottom of a bucket may not look like much, but those unsung "silent crew members" have done their part to contribute to the success of the voyage, and they are deserving of respect as they are committed to the deep. The short, but moving "Service for Items No Longer Wanted" in the *Book of Common Prayer* is an appropriate accompaniment to the disposal procedure. The crew is assembled on deck, and as the container is emptied over the side, the skipper calls out, "Three cheers for our noble leavings!" and the crew responds with lusty huzzahs.

**Jib (Genoa)**

Jib made from pressed meat. Not recommended in warm climates.

**Jib-boom**

"Jib-boom, Jib-boom." Popular hit song of the 1950's, originally recorded by Billy Buddy and the Logarithms.

**Jibe**

Course change which causes the boom to sweep rapidly across the cockpit; also, frequent type of comment made by observers of this maneuver.

**Jury Rig**

An emergency arrangement of sails, lines, spars, etc., usually put together in a period of temporary insanity.

# K

**Ketch**

Disagreeable clause in boat-purchase contract.

*Knot (Advanced)*

| | |
|---|---|
| **Knot** | Any connection between two or more ropes, involving a number of loops, ties, and twists, and having the property that the link cannot be parted or broken in any way or through any means, other than by severing it with a knife, except if it is subjected to steady stress in the course of normal use. There are dozens of highly specialized nautical knots, of which the most common are the half-snarl, the fisherman's snag, the trip-knot, the reef tangle, the rat's foot, the lubber's loop, and the fouline. A seaman who really knows his ropes is referred to as a "knut," a "knerd," a "kninny," or a "knumbskull." |

# L

| | |
|---|---|
| **Latitude and Longitude** | A series of imaginary lines on the earth's surface drawn at intervals parallel to the Equator (latitude) or the poles (longitude) as an aid to navigation. Since they are invisible, many mariners find them of limited usefulness. |
| **Lazaret** | Although by no means all, or even a majority, of sailboat owners are superstitious, by longtime custom a small shrine, called a lazaret, is maintained in the stern of most sailboats. It is basically a locker, with a watertight cover, and it contains what might best be described as an amulet or "juju." This consists of a barbecue grill (representing harvest and the hunt) securely wrapped in 20 to 30 feet of depth-sounding line (symbolizing safe passage through shallow waters), and in turn knotted to several rubber bumpers (symbolizing protection from collisions) with the rope of a small anchor (a symbol of peaceful anchorages). Exact practice varies from boat to boat, but snorkels and face masks (representing the recreational aspects of the sea) are sometimes jammed into the barbecue grill, |

a plastic bucket and a mop (symbolizing cleanliness) are tied to the anchor, and a lantern with a dead battery (a reminder of the cruelty of fate) is placed in the bucket.

**Leadership**     In maritime use, the ability to keep persons on board ship without resorting to measures which substantially violate applicable state and federal statutes.

**Lead Line**     A block of lead at the end of a length of rope which is thrown over the side to determine depth. If it bounces, the course should be changed at once.

**Leak**     A situation calling for LEADERSHIP.

**Leeward**     Pronounced "Lourdes," or shortened to "loo." The direction in which objects, liquids, and other matter may be thrown without risk of reencountering them in the immediate future.

**Lifeboat**     The only known class of vessel which, upon going aboard, an individual thereby increases rather than decreases his chances of survival.

**Life Preserver**     Any personal flotation device that will keep an individual who has fallen off a vessel above water long enough to be run over by it or another rescue craft.

**Lubber**     Or landlubber, an odd rendition of "land-lover." Derogatory slang for persons unfamiliar with boats and uncomfortable in and around them. Modern brain research has indicated that the speech defect which leads some individuals to substitute *b* for *v* may be a symptom of a severe, and hitherto unrecognized, form of brain damage associated with inner-ear dislocations caused by long periods spent pitching, rolling, rocking, and swaying.

*Life Preserver (A.S.P.C.A. Approved)*

*Mooring (Unsuccessful)*

# M

**Marina**  Commercial dock facility. Among the few places, under admiralty law, where certain forms of piracy are still permitted, most marinas have up-to-date facilities for the disposal of excess amounts of U.S. currency that may have accumulated on board ship, causing a fire hazard.

**Mean Low Water**  A phenomenon, probably mythical, first reported by mariners in the sixteenth century, in which some coastal waters at extreme low tide make slapping and burbling noises that sound to the crews of boats passing through them like "You call yourself a sailor? A clam has more brains"; "That's not a boat—that's a barnacle caught on a toothpick"; and other equally malicious remarks.

**Mile (Nautical)**  A relativistic measure of surface distance over water—in theory, 6,076.1 feet. In practice, a number of different values for the nautical mile have been observed while under sail, for example: after 4 P.M., approximately 40,000 feet; in winds of less than 5 knots, about 70,000 feet; and during periods of threatening weather in harbor approaches, around 100,000 feet.

**Mizzen**  1. Itzy-bitzy mazt in zee back of zee boat. 2. Lozt.

**Moon**  Earth's natural satellite. During periods when it displays a vivid blue color, sailing conditions are generally favorable.

**Mooring**  The act of bringing a boat to a complete stop in a relatively protected coastal area in such a fashion that it can be sailed away again in less than one week's time by the same number of people who moored it without heavy equipment and with no more than $100 in repairs.

**Mushroom Anchor** Handy galley accessory that keeps this popular and flavorful fungus from rolling off plates in high seas.

# N

**Naval Architect** Boat designer. Among the best known in modern times are Frank Lloyd Shipwright, Mies van der Roheboat (one of the pioneering architects of the *bauthaus* movement), and Minoru Yachtasaki.

**Navigational Lights** To assist in identification at night, all boats are required to carry various colored lights. Thus, for example, boats for sale display a string of 60-watt bulbs from stem to stern; houseboats are identified by a pair of yellow bug lights, a table lamp, and a small white light in a lantern held by a jockey statuette; and all haunted vessels are bathed in a light green or bluish glow.

**Nylon Rope** A durable synthetic rope that has the curious property that its strength decreases over time in almost exact proportion to the increase in its retail price.

# O

**Offshore** Out of (*a*) sight of land; (*b*) your mind.

**Oil** Thick, viscous substance poured by sailors on troubled waters in former times, but now more frequently poured on troubled beaches, troubled marshes, and troubled seabirds.

**Oilskin** Irritating epidermal condition suffered by boat owners who work on diesel engines.

**Overboard**    No longer on board ship—usually used in reference to a person who has fallen off one. One of the limited number of circumstances when disembarkation from a boat implies a shortening rather than a lengthening of the life span of the individual involved.

# P

**Passage**    Basically, a voyage from point A to point B, interrupted by unexpected landfalls or stopovers at point K, point Q, and point Z.

**Passenger**    A form of movable internal ballast which tends to accumulate on the leeward side of sailboats once sea motions commence.

**Perpetual Motion**    An "impossible" state, in which, once set in motion, an object continues to move forever, defying gravity and friction. All sailboats display perpetual motion. No one knows how this can be, but this interesting subject—and many other fascinating topics—are addressed in the popular book, *Yachts of the Gods?*, which suggests that sailing was taught to earthmen in ancient times by spiteful visitors from outer space in return for having been given spinach, the concept of original sin, and the mumps.

**Pier**    Harbor landing place that goes *crack* or *crunch* when hit.

**Points**    Traditional units of angular measurement from the viewpoint of someone on board a vessel. They are: *Straight ahead of you, right up there; Just a little to the right of the front; Right next to that thing up there; Between those two things; Right out there, look; Over that round doohickey; Off the right corner; Back over there;* and *Right behind us.*

**Porthole**
A glass-covered opening in the hull designed in such a way that when closed (while at sea) it admits light and water, and when open (while at anchor) it admits light, air, and insects (except in Canadian waters, where most species are too large to gain entry in this manner).

**Pratique**
Technical maritime term for customs procedure on entering foreign waters. When passing through customs, particulary in the tropics—the most common foreign destination for American pleasure craft—it is customary to display a small amount of that country's official currency in a conspicuous place and to transfer it to the officer who examines the boat's documents during the parting handshake. A nice sharp slap as the captain effects the transfer shows he cares about appearances. And it is by no means out of place for the skipper to add a friendly word or two, such as "Here, Sambo, this is for *you*. Why don't you go out and buy yourself some joy juice and get stupid?" Incidentally, these inspectors are justly proud of their educational attainments, and the savvy boat owner can win some fast friends by remarking with surprise and admiration on their ability to read and write.

**Privileged Vessel**
The vessel which in a collision was "in the right." If there were witnesses, the owner could bring an admiralty court case—known as a "wet suit" or a "leisure suit"—against the owner of the other boat, and if he proves "shiplash," he could collect a tidy sum. *See* SEA LAWYER.

**Propeller**
Underwater winch designed to wind up at high speed any lines or painters left hanging over the stern.

**Psychology at Sea**
Shipboard therapists deal with many psychoses, ranging from marimania to the Lord Nelson complex.

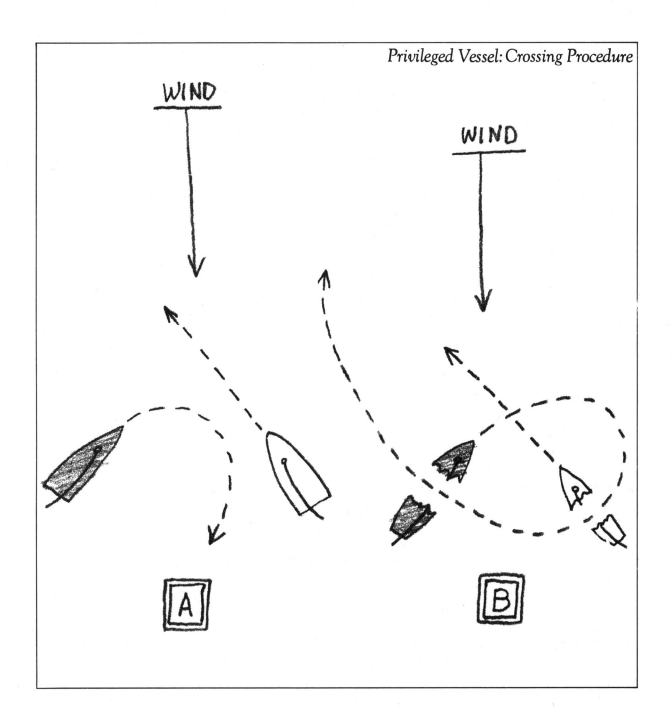

| | |
|---|---|
| **Punt** | 1. Small square-nosed dinghy. 2. To row around in a small square-nosed dinghy. 3. To decide not to row a-round in a small square-nosed dinghy. |

# Q

| | |
|---|---|
| **Quahog** | A large saltwater clam that lives in a shell composed of two joined ashtrays. |
| **Quantum Periodic Galley Table** | A compact piece of fold-up or fold-down furniture, usually built in and/or bolted down, often found in cabins of small sailboats. It has the peculiar characteristic of spontaneously changing state from a tablelike form to a shrunken, collapsed form in an unpredictable manner which modern physics is still at a loss to explain. |
| **Quarantine** | Traditional four-masted plague ship. |
| **Quarter** | Basic gradation of direction as seen from the aft portion of a boat. Thus, for example, a buoy seen at a 45-degree angle off the left of the boat would be 27 cents off the port quarter, tacks included. |
| **Queeg** | Affectionate slang term for ship's captain. |

# R

| | |
|---|---|
| **Racing** | Popular nautical contact sport. |
| **Radar** | Extremely realistic kind of electronic game often found on larger sailboats. Players try to avoid colliding with "blips," which represent other sailboats, large cargo vessels, and supertankers. |

Racing: Grounds for Protest #74

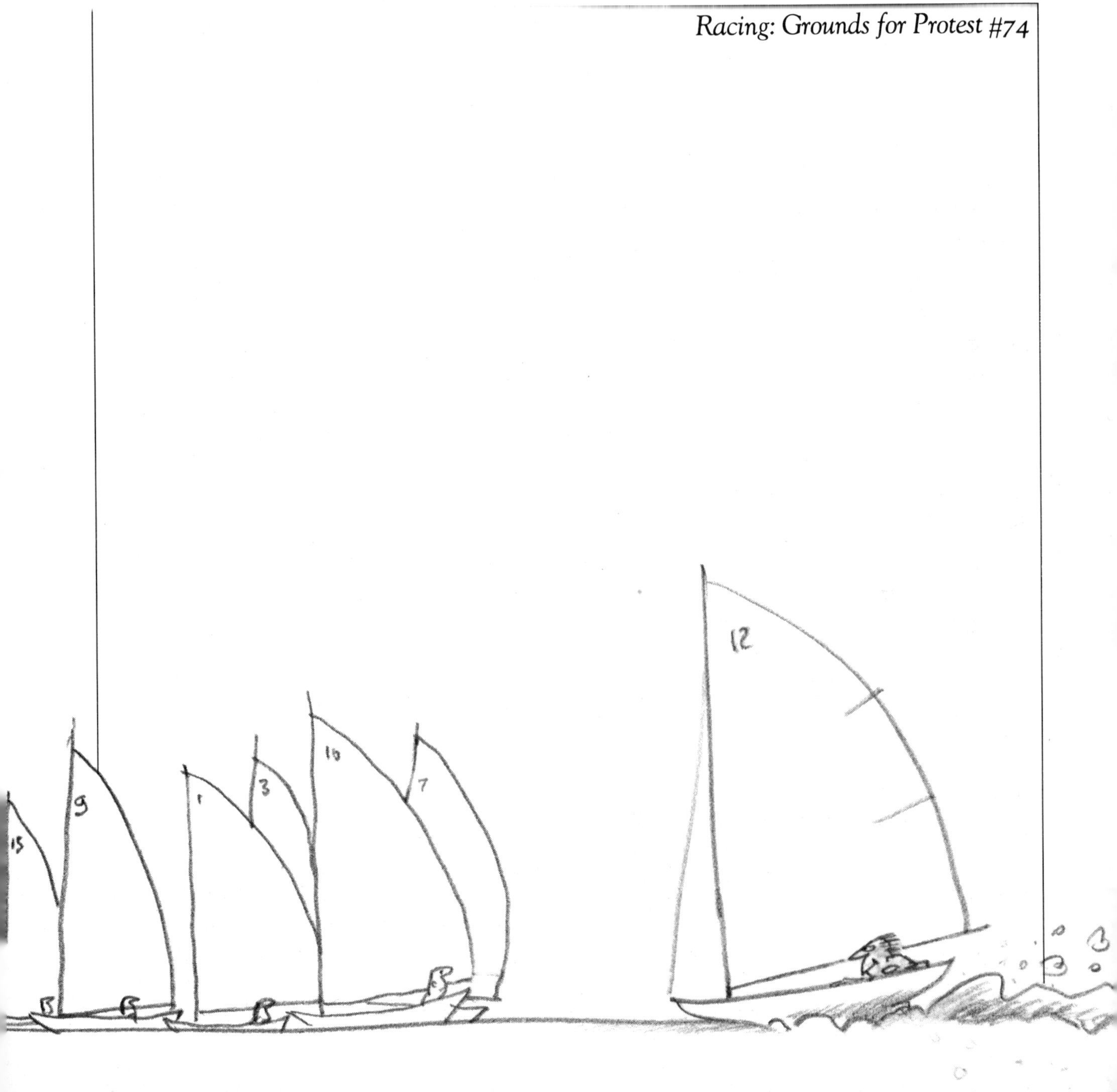

| | |
|---|---|
| **Rapture of the Deep** | Also known as nautical narcosis. Its symptoms include an inability to use common words, such as *up, down, left, right, front,* and *back,* and their substitution with a variety of gibberish which the sufferer believes to make sense; a love of small, dark, wet places; an obsessive desire to be surrounded by possessions of a nautical nature, such as lamps made from running lights and tiny ship's wheels; and a conviction that objects are moving when they are in fact standing still. This condition is incurable. |
| **Red Right Returning** | Best known of a series of mnemonic phrases designed to help sailors remember critical pieces of nautical information. There are many others, like: cold cod cakes can cause catarrh; binnacle, barnacle, baggy wrinkle, boo!; the flounder in zany pajamas swam quickly by the crabby gravlax; and knead a reever, carve a thole. |
| **Regatta** | Jimmy "the Fid" Regatta was generally recognized as the "Codfather" or "Skippo di tutti Skippi" of the shadowy Costa Nostra organized marine-crime family in the northeastern U.S. in the 1950's. Operating out of Newport, R.I., Regatta ran a number of illegal enterprises, including boat-loansharking, the old shellfish game, the sale of adulterated Dramamine, and the protection racket (sailors who frequented the waters of Buzzards Bay in those years remember being approached by seagoing thugs who would chew on toothpicks and drawl insolently, "Nice looking yach-it you got there. It sure would be a shame if a drawbridge closed on it.") A brutal man more noted for his animal cunning than his intellectual capacity, Regatta penned a minor footnote in American legal history when, in an appearance before a Senate committee, he somewhat unexpectedly "took the Third," declining to testify "on |

Rhumb Line (Schematic)

de grounds dat soldiers may be quartered in my home in time of peace widout my consent." Shortly after allegedly fixing the Newport to Eleuthera Race of 1961, the notorious "lobster mobster" came to a predictable end. His removal coincided with rumors that suggested that as recreational boating displaced the traditional fishing industry, a new breed of criminal had come to the area. Rather surprisingly, Jimmy Regatta's body was found buried in a sand trap on the long dogleg par 5 at the exclusive Ball Point Golf Club, and several of his confederates—prior to their disappearance—received mysterious "black balls" marked on pages torn from the *Social Register*. There was talk for a while of a "Madras Mafia," but if it does exist, it is exceptionally discreet.

| | |
|---|---|
| **Relative Motion** | The motion of one boat in relation to another on which the first is converging. If direct convergence occurs, one or both of the boats may develop downward motion. |
| **Rhumb Line** | Shipboard dance similar in some respects to the conga line. |
| **Ropes** | The various kinds of rigging on a boat are extremely sensitive to abuse. *Never call them "ropes."* There is no aspect of sailing in which a novice can more quickly display his ignorance and lack of respect for nautical usage than this, and unless you want a nasty burn the next time you handle "that rope there" or a sharp slap in the face from the end of a miffed hawser, you should learn the proper terms. Generally, "your coilage," "your cordship," or "your lineage" are acceptable when making reference to anchor lines, mooring lines, and the like, but if you wish to avoid unnecessarily chafing your gear, it is advisable to address the more essential forms of rigging by |

their proper names: "Mr. Rutherford, this is the Main Halyard, Holder and Raiser of the Mainsail" or "Mrs. Millicent, may I present the Port and Starboard Jib Sheets."

| | |
|---|---|
| **Rudder** | A large, heavy, vertically mounted, hydrodynamically contoured steel plate with which, through the action of a tiller or wheel, it is possible, during brief intervals, to point a sailing vessel in a direction which, due to a combination of effects caused by tide, current, the force and direction of the wind, the size and angle of the waves, and the shape of the hull, it does not wish to go. |
| **Rule of Thumb** | Hitchhiking at sea is both illegal and inadvisable. |
| **Rules of the Road** | Government-published pamphlet outlining the rights and responsibilities of watercraft in giving way to other vessels in potential collision situations. Since its relatively few pages printed on thin paper have a negligible cushioning capability, it is not thought prudent to rely on it too heavily in the event of an impending impact. |

# S

| | |
|---|---|
| **Schooner** | 1. Traditional sail vessel. 2. Traditional ale vessel. |
| **Scuppers** | Customary disembarkation points for prudent rodents. |
| **Seabag** | 1. Canvas sack in which a sailor's gear is carried. 2. Aging mermaid. |
| **Sea Lawyer** | Attorney practicing admiralty law. For the most part, sea lawyers are reputable, but there are still some "Coast Guard cutter-chasers" around making unethical profits off collision cases, and there are a few notorious "mouth trumpets" or "megaphones" for maritime criminal ele- |

ments. If you have any complaints about the behavior of a sea lawyer, contact your local branch of the American Sand Bar Association.

| | |
|---|---|
| **Sea Monster** | Mythical giant sea creature, usually described as snakelike in appearance. Thought by credulous sailors to appear suddenly and gobble up the unwary. Obviously, a preposterous supersti |
| **Sextant** | An entertaining, albeit expensive, device, which, together with a good atlas, is of use in introducing the boatman to many interesting areas on the earth's surface which he and his craft are not within 1,000 nautical miles of. |
| **Ship's Chandler** | For example, *The Big Sloop*, or *Farewell My Lubberly*. |
| **Shipshape** | A boat is said to be shipshape when every object that is likely to contribute to the easy handling of the vessel or the comfort of the crew has been put in a place from which it cannot be retrieved in less than 30 minutes. |
| **Ship-to-Shore Radio** | A combination radio transmitter/receiver that permits captains and crew members to obtain wrong numbers and busy signals while at sea. |
| **Shower** | Due to restricted space, limited water supplies, and the difficulty of generating hot water, showers on board ship are quite different from those taken ashore. Although there is no substitute for direct experience, a rough idea of a shipboard shower can be obtained by standing naked for two minutes in a closet with a large, wet dog. |
| **Small Craft Warnings** | There are a great many of these, and the wise skipper pays close attention to them. Typical are: "Is there supposed to be water in those drawers under the bunks?"; "I think that man on the fishing boat over there wants to talk |

to you"; "All the other boats are going on the other side of that black thing"; "What does it mean when the little needle breaks off and falls to the bottom of the gauge?"; "If those are sea gulls, why aren't they moving?"; "That's funny, that shiny-looking stuff in the water is only right here around the boat"; "Gee, the wheel suddenly got much easier to turn"; "Hmmmmm, you'd think they'd put an island as big as that on the chart"; "Weren't we towing a little boat behind us when we left?"; and "On second thought, I *will* have one of those little pills."

| | |
|---|---|
| **Snub** | To attach one end of a line to a cleat, and, by extension, to treat a person with disdain or contempt by ignoring him or pretending in some manner that he doesn't exist, as, for example, by attaching one end of a line to him. |
| **Spanner Wrench** | One of the most useful tools for engine repair; in some cases, the only suitable tool. Not currently manufactured. |
| **Spinnaker** | An extremely large, lightweight, balloon-shaped piece of sailcloth frequently trailed in the water off the bow in a big bundle to slow the boat down. |
| **Spinnaker Pole** | Jocular term based on ethnic slur used to describe individual who attempts to fly a spinnaker. |
| **Splice** | Method of joining two ropes by weaving together the individual strands of which they are composed. The resulting connection is stronger than any knot. Splicing is something of an art and takes a while to master. You can work on perfecting your technique at home by practicing knitting a pair of socks or a stocking cap out of a pound or so of well-cooked noodles. |
| **Stowing** | A form of temporary caulking in which clothes and personal belongings are jammed into a number of irregu- |

*Spinnaker at Maximum Efficiency*

lar spaces between the inner hull and the cabin for the purpose of absorbing any random moisture, caused by small leaks, etc., which may have collected there.

| | |
|---|---|
| **Suit of Sails** | Sail wardrobes are still mostly white, but some solid colors are beginning to appear, and if Mark La Motte, editor of *Harbors Bazaar* and author of *The Well-Dressed Ship* is right, checks, plaids, and patterns are just around the corner, and we'll soon be seeing a move away from the ''Continental look'' Marconi rig in favor of a return to the baggy tweed or flannel ''Vanderbilt'' style mainsails that were so popular in Newport in the 1920's. |
| **Surf 'n' Turf** | Popular harborside restaurant dish consisting, typically, of a lobster tail and a filet mignon. Other generally accepted terms for this combination are: Angler 'n' Wrangler; Beef 'n' Reef; Maine 'n' Plain; Pound 'n' Sound; Paw 'n' Claw; Loam 'n' Foam; Chap 'n' Trap; Steer 'n' Pier; Kine 'n' Brine; Marine 'n' Bovine; Paddle 'n' Saddle; Oar 'n' Shore; Sand 'n' Brand; Tide 'n' Hide; Dive 'n' Drive; Comber 'n' Roamer; Lasso 'n' Sargasso; Ship 'n' Whip; Boat 'n' Oat; Cud 'n' Scud; Rudder 'n' Udder; Slime 'n' Prime; Scow 'n' Cow; and Ooze 'n' Moos. |
| **Swab** | To effect, with the aid of a mop, a sponge, or some similar device, the even distribution of a mixture of seawater, dirt, food particles, ash, and other foreign matter over the entire deck, cockpit, and cabin. |
| **Swimming** | A form of solo waterborne navigation, ordinarily practiced over short distances, whose expense, compared with sailing, is negligible, since the most costly item—the boat—is dispensed with entirely. |

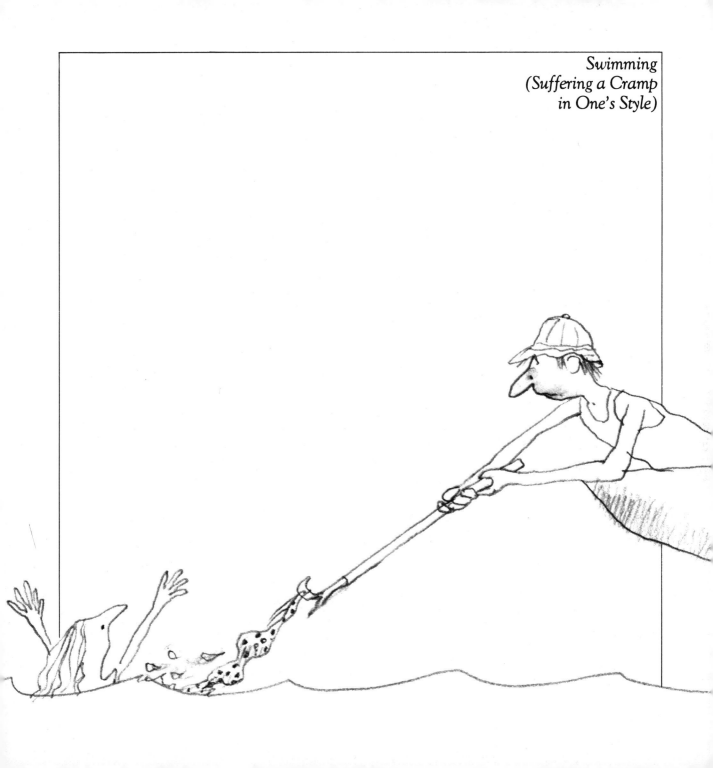

# T

| | |
|---|---|
| **Tack** | To shift the course of a sailboat from a direction far to the right, say, of the direction in which one wishes to go, to a direction far to the left of it. |
| **Teredo** | A wormlike saltwater organism, actually a mollusk. The only known creature whose fondness for traditional all-wooden sailing vessels matches that of their owners'. |
| **Thwart** | Thmall, hard lump of thkin found on handth of thailorth who fail to take precauthions when handling frogth. |
| **Tides** | Rise and fall of coastal waters. There are two tides daily on weekdays, one on Saturday, and none on Sunday, Harbor Day, Spinnukah, Swabber Day, Clam Wednesday, and Farragut's Birthday. For tides in your area, be sure to consult your local tide tables. For example, someone leaving Groton on the 11:07 (a local tide) has to be at Block Island by 6:13 to catch the outbound Long Island Sound tide (a notoriously unreliable flow), and regardless of point of origin or destination, everyone in the Northeast has to change at Sandy Hook. Even if the water is running smoothly, planning is essential. Dredging operations sometimes result in delays, and tides are occasionally canceled without notice. Incidentally, as this book went to press, the Coast Guard was considering designating certain tides as "smoking" or "no smoking"—call your local boating association for details. |
| **Toe** | Stub your "toe"? Well then, it's time to brush up on your nomenclature! In nautical terms, a toe is a *catchcleat* or *snagtackle*. A few others: head—*boomstop*; leg—*bruisefast*; and hand—*blistermitten*. |

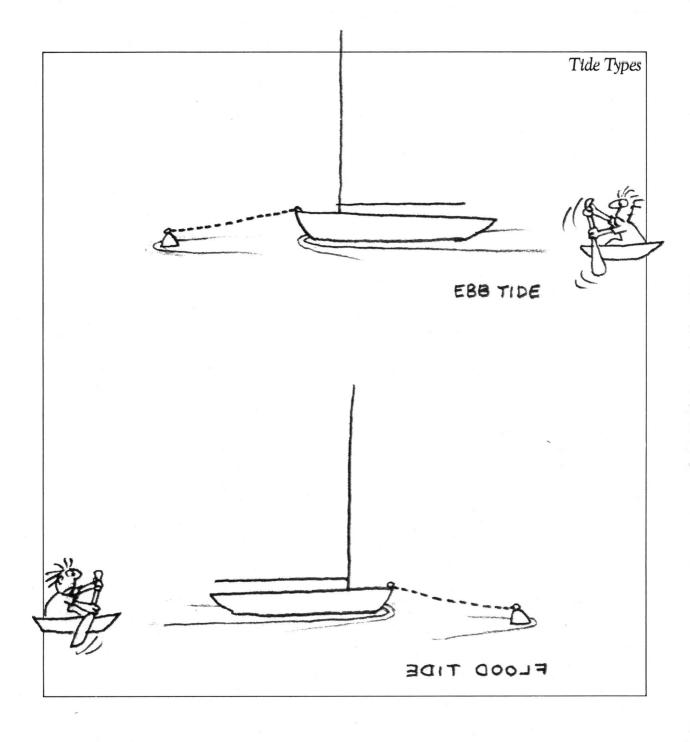

Uniform

FIG. 1 AMATEUR          FIG. 2 PROFESSIONAL

| | |
|---|---|
| **Trailering** | Transporting a boat to dockside on a car-trailer. One of the few situations in which a boat owner not aboard his boat is in substantially the same peril as when he is on it. |
| **True North** | The direction in which the geographic North Pole lies, as distinguished from the directions in which compass needles point, which range from Magnetic North to Sort of North, Northish, East, West, and South. |

# U

| | |
|---|---|
| **Uniform** | As worn by yacht club members and other shore hazards, a distinctive form of dress intended to be visible at a distance of at least 50 meters which serves to warn persons in the vicinity of the long winds and dense masses of hot air associated with these tidal bores. |
| **U.S. Government Publications** | The U.S. government publishes a number of pamphlets and booklets of interest to mariners. Among the most useful are the Annual Tax Tables, which provide a list—updated weekly—of all state and federal tariffs applicable to boat owners; "Tax Sale Ho!", which describes the process of seizing an individual's watercraft to satisfy liens; and "Sure You Survived a Shipwreck—But Will You Survive an Audit?", an excellent survival manual which contains waterproof tax forms, a comprehensive definition of the one circumstance under which the abandoning of a boat is considered a nontaxable "involuntary disposal of assets," and clearly-written instructions for the marooned sailor on how to avoid eventual |

Weighing Anchor:
The Importance of Cooperation

IRS penalties upon rescue by keeping a careful record of fish caught, roots and berries consumed, and other forms of "windfall sustenance in lieu of income."

| | |
|---|---|
| **U.S. Weather Service** | Relying on sophisticated sensing devices which turn pink or blue depending on key meteorological indications, the U.S. Weather Service makes regular radio broadcasts describing changing weather conditions. |

# V

| | |
|---|---|
| **Vang** | Name of German sea dog. |
| **Varnish** | High-fiction coating applied as a gloss over minor details in personal nautical recollections to improve their audience-holding capacity over frequent retellings. |

# W

| | |
|---|---|
| **Wake** | 1. Horizontal track in the water caused by passage of a boat. 2. Ceremony held if that track becomes vertical. |
| **Weather Helm** | Marked tendency of a sailboat to turn into the wind, even when the rudder is centered. This is easily countered by wedging a heavy object against the tiller. *See* CREW. |
| **Weigh Anchor** | To raise the anchor. This odd terminology may derive from the fact that every time the anchor is pulled up—almost always by hand on sailboats—an excellent opportunity is presented to the crew members hauling it up to gain a good working idea of its weight, which is generally considerable and, apart from minute changes caused by corrosion, quite consistent from one weighing to another. |

Still, it is a source of cheer and comfort to many that in a constantly changing nautical environment, 30 or more deadweight pounds of metal are "hanging in there," and this may be why sailors traditionally sing chanteys when pulling them up.

| | |
|---|---|
| **Wharf** | Sound made by Vang when he wishes to be fed. |
| **Whelk** | Sound made by Vang to show that he doesn't like that dry, lumpy dog food you put in his dish. |
| **Whip** | Useful accessory if that dry, lumpy dog food is all you happen to have on board. |
| **Whitecaps** | 1. Agitated, foamy water on the tops of waves. 2. Luggage handlers at seaside hotels. |
| **Winches** | Jocular term for compliant and helpful young ladies on a sailboat. By contrast, women who are serious sailors but dull company are called "windlasses" or "wet bulbs." |
| **Windward** | The direction the wind is coming from, also known as the eye of the wind or the teeth of the wind, and in New Jersey coastal waters, the mouth of the wind. |
| **Wing-and-Wing or Double Wing** | A unique soft-shoe step perfected by the comedy tap-dancing team of Flo and Eddy and first introduced in their 1933 hit, *Mermaid in Heaven*. |

# X

| | |
|---|---|
| **Xebec** | Also, zebec. A small, three-masted Mediterranean sailing vessel, used primarily in commerce in the Middle East, and in Scrabble in North American waters. |

Winch in Operation

The Yacht:
A Source of Serenity
and Peace

# Y

| | |
|---|---|
| **Yacht** | Any recreational craft whose owner or user is not responsible for her upkeep, or whose owner recognizes sufficient tax benefits from his ownership to defray all operating expenses. Also commony used to describe any boat prior to its purchase, and by many boat owners to describe their vessel to persons who have never seen it and are never likely to do so. |
| **Yacht Broker** | Form of coastal marine life found in many harbors in the Northern Hemisphere generally thought to occupy a position on the evolutionary scale above algae, but below the cherrystone clam. |
| **Yardarm** | Horizontal spar mounted in such a way that when viewed from the cockpit, the sun is always over it. |
| **Yawl** | Southern version of *ahoy*. |

# Z

| | |
|---|---|
| **Zee** | The Dutch have made significant contributions to boating safety in their tiny country by draining coastal areas long favored by Netherlands yachtsmen and converting them to farmland. The fleets of little *mudtfrigjates* scudding through the fields of ripening turnips and Brussels sprouts are a peculiar but colorful sight, and although some complain that the swish of plant tops along the hull and the squelch of rubber tires in mud are no substitute for the slap of waves and the tang of salt, there is no denying that the unfortunate sailor who capsizes is better off in Davy Jones's larder than in his locker! |

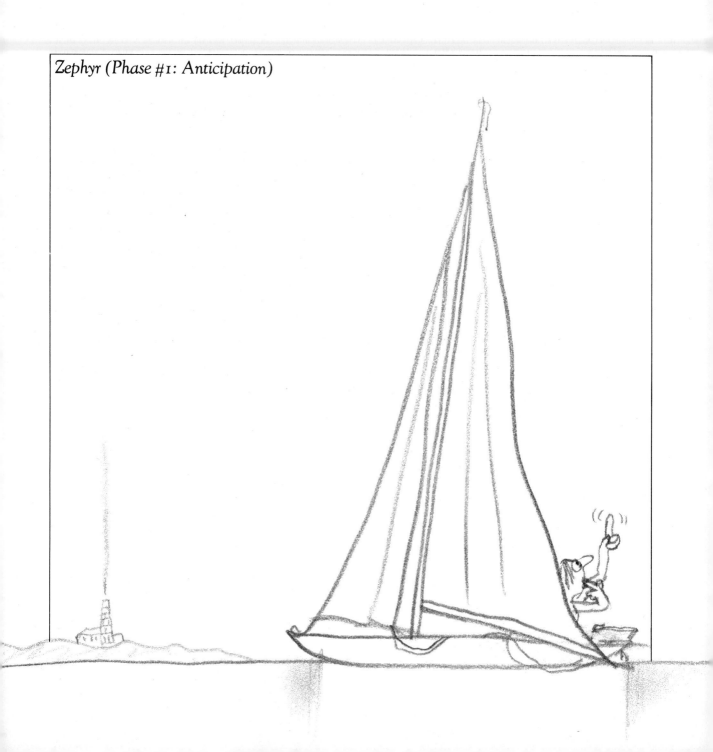

*Zephyr (Phase #1: Anticipation)*

| | |
|---|---|
| **Zenith** | One of a number of odd and probably meaningless terms used by adherents of Celestial Navigation, a peculiar cult whose members profess to believe that it is possible to tell where you are by consulting mystical "tables" and peering at the stars and planets through an instrument that looks like something abandoned by the dental profession around the turn of the century. Though rarely dangerous, celestial navigators—or "starries" as they are sometimes called—are avid proselytizers, and sailors who don't want to be pressed to join in their odd rituals are advised to give them a wide berth at twilight when they gather on deck and mumble numbers at one another. |
| **Zephyr** | Warm, pleasant breeze. Named after the mythical Greek god of wishful thinking, false hopes, and unreliable forecasts. |
| **Zubenelgenubi** | Navigational star. *See* ACHERNAR. |